Drive me crazy

Have fun with your partner trying

dirty talking

Jenna Corey

Drive me crazy

Have fun with your partner trying dirty talking

Jenna Corey

reader. Under no circumstances will any legal responsibility or blame be held against the publisher for any reparation, damages, or monetary loss due to the information herein, either directly or indirectly.

Respective authors own all copyrights not held by the publisher.

The information herein is offered for informational purposes solely, and is universal as so. The presentation of the information is without contract or any type of guarantee assurance. The trademarks that are used are without any consent, and the publication of the trademark is without permission or backing by the trademark owner. All trademarks and brands within this book are for clarifying purposes only and are the owned by the owners themselves, not affiliated with this document

Table of Contents

Introduction

Both men and women love to hear what their partner wants to do for them, or what will be done to them before it's done. Hearing the words moaned, screamed, whispered, or growled heightens the sensations and can take the love making to a whole new level.

However, dirty talking is not as "easy" as people make it seem. It's not just a matter of using every swear word the sailors taught you. There is an art and even a science to shocking the senses. Effectively dirty talking is a careful balancing act of expressing desire, of smart communication between two different lovers, and letting yourself feel the emotion of the moment.

In this guide, you will learn exactly how to talk dirty and how to do it right. You will discover what dirty talking is, the science of it, as well as the art of putting your own creative spin on the age-old hobby of talking your lover off. It takes you, step by step, from getting in the mood, during foreplay, during love making, to afterglow. You will know what to say and how to say it in every situation. And more importantly, you will be comfortable and sound confident when you talk dirty.

In moments of passion, you have a strange desire to talk dirty but you don't know how to do it, you feel awkward and you don't know how your partner could react. Your friends do it and you even see it in the movies, but when you try it you feel stuck, and those times when you did it you felt uncomfortable, almost stupid.

Many people experience this situation, they would like but cannot, they feel that they are missing out a lot of fun but they do not know how to do it or even how to learn it, since it is not an easy topic to ask others for advice. Some other people instead already use dirty talking with their partner, but they would like to go beyond the usual sentences and learn how to master this art.

That's why we decided to create a book that can help anyone quickly and without having to deal with embarrassing conversations.

This book is not just a dirty talk manual full of many practical examples, it is a complete guide that will accompany you step by step in improving all aspects of your sex life, nothing will be left to chance.

Even if you think it's impossible for you and you feel strange even just imagining yourself in pronouncing certain sentences and words, this book will help you to be an expert in dirty talking.

Chapter one

What is dirty talk?

Though it may sound like a ridiculous question to ask, even for some girls, they still desire just a tiny extra info about which filthy speaking is focused on until they dare to check it out. That really is only part of human nature, yet until we're eager to try out something, you wish to be certain we are proficient in it first. That really is the way you're feeling. Before you dare to wow your man with a few dirty talks during intercourse to ship him on the border. The very last thing you would like to do is wholly kibosh a sexy moment and wind up buying an entire doofus. That is not likely to happen for you.

Thus, what's dirty-talk? Well, it's simply like it sounds. It really is bedroom language that individuals use to convey with our wants, needs, and desires to each other. On occasion, it's even utilized to convey an idea or used like a cocktail. There is really not only a special way to specify dirty-talk since it differs for several couples.

Although it sounds daunting right now when you find out how to filthy talk and the way to feel comfortable with it, both you and your man will develop your form of bedroom conversation, which may send you over the border.

Dirty conversation is fun! It is an excellent way to enhance your sexual activity life also to produce matters in the bed room heat up much farther. Nothing is as sexy like a breathy announcement said from the heat of this moment. It's time you just got aboard with this trend and also made it a basic for both you and your own man!

This is the biggest difficulty that girls are when it concerns dirty discussion - that they cannot conquer the anxiety. Yes, it's nervewracking to eventually become outspoken for its very first time at the sack once you normally are not utilized for it, yet that really is really where all of us flourish. After we're taken out of our comfort zones, which is once we really begin alive and really begin loving sex for exactly what it's worth.

You can not anticipate your sexual life to flourish in case you're always staying inside your own boundaries. Understanding how to experiment somewhat out of these bounds is actually exciting and certainly will result in more pleasant sessions at the bed room.

Thus just how would you overcome the anxiety? It will not happen overnight. The ideal method to begin to get convenient with filthy conversation is always to start with sexting.

Sexting entails utilizing your telephone to ship filthy texting to your guy. They could be anywhere from pg-rated all of the way to mature words that are rated. I'd urge to always start light off. Following that, you may begin to produce things to get warmer as you become convenient. Start by telling him just how far you really cannot wait to watch him or her later how sexy you really imagine he's. This can allow one to receive more comfy with the thought of increasing the speech and also utilizing a few raunchier language. Once sex ting is just like a cinch, then it is a great thought to start talking more throughout sex. The ideal approach to start is to decorate your guy or maybe to inform him exactly what seems good since it's happening. Following that, you can get accustomed to with your voice throughout sex, which is likely to definitely make upcoming bouts of foul conversation come far more naturally and seamlessly for your requirements personally, leading to fabulous bedroom conversation that brings both you and your individual more and more excited.

Do not worry when the nervousness proceeds to last. You might be doing something which isn't the standard for you; it is just natural that you're likely to feel uncomfortable. Do not fret though, practice makes perfect and the longer you can do it, the easier it'll be!

Thus, now that you're prepared and feeling a little more confident with some sex ting examples and mild foul talk during intercourse, everything goes next?

Well, obviously, you're working towards an objective of making a different love speech involving you and your own man. To carry out it, you want to begin filthy talking from the very first place, as, let us face it, this is all up for one get started.

Dirty-talk is a lot sexier; if girls take action, yes, it will be sexy if a man starts doing this; however, he probably won't take part inside until you choose the guide; therefore, it's all up for one to start it.

To assist you to begin filthy talking in bed tonight, then attempt these 5 hints to night!

1. Be very first. You do not need to seem rehearsed, and also you do not want to seem too practiced. Additionally, that you never want to seem just like you studied this, and also you don't wish to express something which does not pertain to a own man. Say something that's for him and him. It is likely to ensure it is a very unique and unique experience for the two of you this manner.

2. Be convinced. This might be the largest hint of all time. In case you're perhaps not confidence, he is going to have the ability to share with, and it should come across as awkward and odd. Do not get this happen. Make certain of what it is you will state and believe it.

3. Maintain it in the bay. When items are heating, it may be simple to carry things just a touch too much better. Maintain the reigns on and ensure they stay to a certain degree. Do not get in front of yourself or rush matters!

4. Enjoy pleasure. In case you are not enjoying it, then he will have the ability to tell. Make certain you are having a great time and let loose with filthy conversation. It's assumed to be more fun!

5. Be yourself. Men may not be the sharpest knives at the shop occasionally, nor pick upon exactly what our subtitles are about; however, they will tell when you aren't yourself.

At the finish of this all, you merely need dirty conversation to become more fun. Additionally, it really should not be something you truly feel pressured to doing something which you're not confident or comfortable with. If you ever feel some period of jealousy or disquiet, your man will probably pick up about it, and he'll feel uncomfortable.

Fantastic guideline to keep in mind:

"When it seems terrible on mind, do not state it outside loud."

If you're looking overly tough to think of something to state, then it will seem unnatural and rehearsed. As an alternative, make an effort to state things which can come up at the present time. This really is when you're in the authentic, and that really is when you will be in your wildest because of him personally.

Don't forget to have some fun and also to love it! Dirty conversation is enjoyable, and it's something which may badly amp up your bedroom drama and eventually become something special between the 2 of you. You've mastered the sack abilities and lingerie. You understand to your man, also at the act please yourself. You're great in the bag; however, you wish to go a notch higher. It's time to decide to try dirty talking. You may possibly have awarded it a go a couple of times; however, it might well not have gone also. Things you desire is really a idle girl's lead to dirty talking.

On the lookout for newcomer hints?

Though there are numerous hints and hints of filthy talking out there, the majority are obscure or completely immaterial for a lady with one's center to talk dirty but have certainly not figured out the way to yet. I read a post compiled by Dana Myers, the creator of booty parlor, to the advice and shortcuts for talking dirty. Dana an authority in the area and also a sexual goddess developed a set of hints and hints for novices that would like to simply take their sexual lives towards the following level.

Baby measures

To start, you ought to be aware of very well what filthy speaking is. In accordance with Dana, we frequently consider filthy conversation, and the first thing that comes to their heads isn't might never do this' as it seems really debilitating. For those who have perfected seduction utilizing human body motions, your own eyes and your smile and your grin, and then you'll be able to just as readily apply the mouth area verbally - to get the very same. Women are usually glossy and tender, but to become always a dirty talker, you also must practice being gloomy, raunchy also to some degree, slutty and racy. From the sack, anything else goes.

Therefore, how will you get it?

An ideal filthy talk is really a mixture of everything you state, the way you're saying the mood you put, and the corresponding body activities. You might need to become open, and also, in the ideal mindset, it may well not get the job done. It'd be foolish, even dumb, to aim to discuss dirty whilst laughing or while overly severe. A fantastic strategy is to explain what it is that you do because that's straightforward or educate your partner exactly what you need to perform. One other fantastic type of filthy conversation also has to describe your feelings and emotions through the warmth of this moment, followed closely by physical moves and compliments for the own man.

Start easy

One huge mistake that most men and women create is copying what pornography stars state, word by word. It comes off too extreme and really biased. "It's excellent to be," says Dana, "start simple, using phrases like "Touch my skin with your fingers" or "Sting my throat" Dana believes the very best thing a newcomer has to do in order to simplify learning how to talk dirty would always be to find an erotica publication written specifically to get a newcomer. The guide will probably possess hints, thoughts, and guides that'll direct a girl from abc to perfection at a quick moment. Women's magazines and sites supply us with some really crucial advice we might well not find somewhere else. They show suggestions and perspectives that help them know men and the way to manage them or them. The majority of women frequently need to take care of the embarrassment that includes the very first two or three times they decide to try talking dirty. It's probable your man enjoys dirty talking just as far as you personally; however, someone always needs to get the first movement. Livening up things in the bedroom isn't too hard; indeed, you only need a couple pointers. Below are a number of tips and also don'ts of dirty-talk you will see beneficial.

The do's:

- inform him how amazing he could be. Men are suckers for praise. Allow him to feel amazing about his operation, his abilities, and also his entire body. This ought to go together with everything he needs to do. You ought to make telling him exactly what to do, the way you can please you, and also steps exactly to make you're feeling great an integral part of dirty-talk.

- exactly like everything else, sexual assurance is something you need to construct - before you jump right into bed. This could comprise sexts, flirting, and word-play before childbirth. The fantastic thing about the fact of the fact that it sets the pace and also the mood for that which is ahead of time.

- the very easiest way to speak filthy and let it flow obviously would always be to tell your guy the way you're feeling. Moaning and telling him just how beautiful you're atmosphere indoors - that really is an excellent way to get started. This sort of filthy conversation might be simple "Yes! Yes!

Yes!" or it may really go "It seems really good," "Oh, I like that, I really like it!"

- naughtiness may be the trick to talking dirty exactly the ideal way. Naughtiness, nevertheless, is dependent upon what free and open you and your individual will be to each other. While building assurance does take some time, however, finally, you may.

The don'ts:

- do not try overly much or overdo it. Everything you might have noticed porn celebrities do might appear realistic, but should you shout out all of the filthy phrases you can consider, such a spoils the mood. It's ideal for keeping it simple but fair compared to risk spoiling the mood.

- do not keep this up if your partner isn't engrossed. That really is where sex ting and word-play before childbirth demonstrates essential. You are going to have the ability to tell if a man is playing together or he's resisting.

Are men into women that talk dirty from the sack? In case they're, how will you learn how to talk dirty exactly the ideal manner - as like everything else, how dirty-talk may be the ideal thing to occur to a sexual life, or it could possibly be the worst. All of us are a fascinating lot, are not we?

Most women that I've talked to lately seeing cluttered talking state they like to please their spouses in the bed room; however, that the best fear many have is losing hands. I accumulated transforming from the prim and proper lady to a complete slut, and naughty girl inside the bedroom is hard; however, it's achievable.

The most important thing about filthy talking is that it's about communicating. Talking dirty is conveying your own feelings and wants and teaching your partner exactly what to accomplish. For suitable communication, you've got to be relaxed and free and understand that your partner well enough to see the things which turn them and those you ought to avoid.

The best tip I can provide you would be to begin gradually - there's not any requirement to push and behave as a porn superstar in your own very first effort as it can backfire upon your own head. Most girls will realize that using certain phrases and words can be embarrassing and could feel bashful about any of it, however whenever that they find how simple it's to open up and go to town. When I pointed out earlier, communication will be the trick to getting everything you also desire, it's far easier to get a lady to talk dirty compared to for some guy to.

I must also state that speaking about filthy talking and sharing some lusty dreams you have can assist you to know what your partner wants and also him to understand exactly what to expect and exactly what to accomplish. While I had been researching about this topic, I spoke to a range of girls and never get the time and effort to inquire men exactly what they consider talking dirty - like most different matters regarding gender. The outcome is there are things they wish to mention or matters that they desire their spouses to accomplish, but they never get them.

Girls who've left the work and mastered dirty speaking please their guys a lot better compared to people that are quiet during intercourse. I requested a few boys also for their remarks about filthy speaking, and nearly every person I inquired confessed being caused by one type of filthy conversation or another. The most important thing is, guys, anticipate dirty talking - even when it's only moaning and swearing - out of you, your ex. What do you want to do about any of it?

Chapter two

Where to get ideas

You may be reading this as your partner has voiced a fascination in hearing gloomy words at the heat of the fire. You may possibly have searched out this publication as you're the person who wants those sweet nothings. Maybe you wish to spice up your sexual life, or you may be simply interested as to the reason your partner wants to talk a lot during intercourse. You may be a wonderful dirty talker that needs a brand new idea or 2, or perhaps you are simply in the mood to brush up on your own skills that are naughty. No matter the rationale, you've chosen the ideal approach to get things you require! Discussing filthy has gotten so much part of our sexual culture; it has spawned interviews, surveys, forums, books, and research. In reality, earlier, it had been called "dirty conversation," the craft of saying sexual matters to an enthusiast with all the goal to excite needed a scientific name: lagnolalia. There is a very good reason for all of this technological interest. Over 80 percent of our sexual life occurs within our minds, meaning fantasy, memory, and appetite are a few of the very effective driving forces behind what we are doing behind closed doors. Various studies have revealed that at the time you actually become physical with your partner, the mind continues to be contributing up to your encounter. Therefore why don't you select the filthy conversation? This has been at the trunk of mind throughout the day-long anyway! As stated by aline p. Zoldbrod, PhD, the author of over just a couple novels on naughtiness, sexy speak to your partner not merely revs play between your sheets, but enhances your own life in ways you never have envisioned. It creates your partner feel great to understand how excited you're, and also, your delight makes them feel as the very best fan on the earth. Which may explain why cluttered conversation allows you to tingle in all of the ideal places, however, it will not explain the naughtiest dirty conversation may be the most hottest. It's one thing to say "fuck" and also find yourself a grin, but it's another to share with your partner exactly the way you wish to fuck them in the most graphic terms it's possible to see right now. The dirtier what, the higher. What is up with this? One term: taboo. By the time we're small kiddies, we're instructed to not say dirty words. Saying naughty matters just isn't exactly what good boys or girls perform. Mentioning that taboo using a partner who makes you feel just like you are breaking the rules and that subsequently causes you to feel adventurous. After the bedroom door shuts behind you and also people dirty words come from your own mouth, your social conventions disappear. You might seem just like angry, and you will possibly get somewhat paranoid and wonder exactly what could occur if anybody, god forbid, discovered you talking like that! You will possibly find flustered rather than have the ability to speak above a whisper. That is when you understand you've only busted down a barrier that you will possibly not have understood was there at the first location. The finest filthy talk pops open a much wider doorway with an extremely crucial question: in case you're able to talk dirty in bed, then everything else would you do? Discussing filthy unlocks doors that you never knew were not there! Explicit conversation is actually a confidence-booster, too. Not merely does this make him alluring to listen about the situations that you wish regarding him, but in addition, it provides you the pride of focusing on how meticulously you've flipped your spouse. The more naughtier you talk, the more sexier you're feeling. This sexiness will not disappear once you leave the sack, and also the confidence that you pull out of this spills over into whatever else you're doing. Most of all, talking dirty provides you with the opportunity to voice whatever you actually desire during sex, if with lively speech or dull and to the purpose in any event it increases your probability of sexual gratification. Zoldbrod highlights that the advantage of foul conversation: it is an established actuality that women who talk in their sexual demands have sex more frequently and therefore are somewhat more joyful.

The most significant part

Before you embark upon the experience of studying how to speak dirty for your partner, maintain the most significant part of sex at heart. No, it isn't the technique during intercourse that one oh my god movement which produces everybody else you've ever lurks beg for longer. It isn't the dirty conversation -- though we'd really like to state this may be by far the main things you can perform during intercourse, it surely does rank a close 2nd. What rankings first? Intimacy. Pure, honest familiarity. There are lots of definitions of familiarity, however, in regards to romantic connections, it boils down to exactly the identical. Intimacy may be your sensation of being near some person, which warmth and relaxation that comes in knowing somebody well. It's a lot more than sex -- in reality, you can have familiarity without sex in any way. Intimacy is your psychological link and answers you've got to a partner. The latest fall is compared to this cool heat, which comes when familiarity is demanded.

Becoming confident with your partner, desperate to please, and also prepared to start a part of him maybe the secret to an excellent sexual life. But that is only the onset of good stuff. As closeness assembles, our inhibitions drop. The more comfortable you feel with your novelty, the more inclined you should adopt every element of it, although people that you may have previously considered taboo. In the middle of deep familiarity, the frightening thing could be enabling. Talking dirty is much like sharing a secret together with your partner, you which only both of you understand and know. Whenever you are out and around in people, showcasing your best face to the earth, nobody, however, your partner knows just how courageous you are able to definitely be. Whenever you face your colleagues or your supervisor or physician or another person, for instance, they don't have any concept about the genuine person that you feel when you're in bed with your companion. Your partner could be the only person that sees all of the hidden sides of you personally. What a joy, knowing there's something really special that only the both of you talk, no one else may guess! Since you learn how to talk dirty, it opens a completely new universe of potential. You may likely know things about your partner that you won't ever envision, and it is a sure bet he is going to know a little about you! Your openness to talk dirty to him shows him just how much you really would like him, and that contributes to improved familiarity between both of you. The closer you are feeling to a partner, the better your sex life will probably be. However, the deepest closeness leaves just a tiny room for shyness, which is where this book is useful. Think you are too bashful for filthy conversation? By the time you are finished reading that, you may not be! All these chapters are made to take you out of the filthy talk principles towards the talking dirty as a specialist, are certain to definitely get the mind racing, your heart pounding...as well as your own mouth at down and dirty gear.

Dirty chat does not always have to become filthy

If you listen to the phrases "dirty talk," what's the first reaction? What should you find from the rear of the mind? Odds are once you consider filthy conversation, your initial idea is something which you've seen from a porn picture. It's extraordinary, perhaps somewhat awkward. Maybe it's really "Out there" you cannot imagine doing in your bedroom. On the flip side, perhaps it's so dirty it turns you around, and that by itself causes you to feel just a little...well, filthy. You may possibly remember a scene or 2 of a woman talking non stop from the dirtiest speech she might muster. Maybe even considering this gets you to blush. However, it functions you at precisely the exact same moment. Once you first start to explore dirty-talk, you are entering a place that has ever been thought of taboo. However, openminded you're, there may be instances when you're feeling somewhat uneasy. However, some would assert that an indication of very good dirty discussion is the fact that it gets you to squirm in the chair!

After all, even in case all of the genders were all comfortable, what is exciting about that? Dirty-talk in that pornography picture may be over the top and corny.

Nevertheless, the dirty talk becomes familiar with through this publication won't seem corny at all -- it'll seem sexy, complicated, and oh so sexy. To put it differently, do not make an effort to take on this pornography celebrity. They have been reading a script, so being fed up with their traces, and true to life isn't just like that. In actual life, you are able to be more alluring than any pornstar! It requires time to make it happen, but so simply take things slow and focus on the fundamentals.

To start with, dirty-talk does not need to be dirty. It is possible to present your joy -- and then rev his engine to redline -- with all the noises that you create. If you descend in joy, it informs him he is doing something right. If you snore because he enters you, then you are telling him just how much you really enjoy how he believes inside you. How you sigh whenever you close your eyes and cave in the impression could make him feel just like a king. The noises that you create, if groaning or yelling or simply heavy-breathing will let him amounts about the way you're feeling and everything you need him to complete. The design of your voice travels a very long way, too. After you whisper in his ear, then your voice is going to likely be roughened and daunted with the fire you are feeling. That is clearly an all-natural response to one's own body. There isn't one thing bogus about this noise that originates from the mouth, along with your fan, will recognize it in how the funniest fires unfold. Though candy amorous words and hardcore raunchy kinds have their own place, sometimes simply whispering a word that is sexy can be more powerful than simply belting it out in the middle of passion. Saying just how much you adore the way he rolls you're good, however, murmuring it in his ear is much better. Lean small kisses down his torso at the same time you whisper you need to taste him. Simple words, nothing cuter -- however, the direction that they have been said, with all the sultry tone of one's voice, will do to light all of his dials. The emphasis you wear specific words may instantly create a feeling of appetite. "contact me," makes it clear at which you desire his hands. "my turn" may possibly be quite a fantastic solution to tell him you need to be on top. "give me" says, undoubtedly, you would like to buy...whatever" it" could be. Get creative with the easy, usual words that you used during sex, and also make use of the accent to get your wishes clear.

Listed below are a couple more "not filthy talk."

Examples:

I think it's great when you touch me.

Immediately, honey. That is it.

Immediately.

Do not stop.

I think it's great whenever you glance at me.

Do this ...and again!

You are so very good at this.

Which makes me melt...

I adore how that you are feeling against your own skin.

Your own body is ideal.

Lay back and let me play you for a short time!

You taste so great.

You make me feel good.

Tell me the way you would like to buy it.

I can not stop shaking... I need you Therefore much better.

You make me hot.

My body feels living!

How can you do these items to Me?

The entire body turns me.

Watch what you are doing if you ask me personally.

Have you got any notion exactly what this Does to me personally?

Try my eyes once you really do That.

I appreciate the items that you are able to perform together with Your palms.

You are so great with your own tongue, Baby.

I have never believed anything similar to this

Before.

Do you believe it? Feel the best way to Made my own entire body react?

This really is one reason I love You.

Seeking his eyes since you possibly state those sexy items is consistently a turnon. Men are extremely visual animals; therefore, if they are able to easily see what they're doing at precisely the exact same time, they have heard the effects of one's voice will probably soon be so much sexier. In addition, they like to discover what's going on inside you, on a psychological level, where it sounds. What buff does not desire to wow his own partner? By looking to your eyes since you state something in their mind, they are able to observe the way you feel, too. The mixture of the physical and the emotional can be a heady one. But that just goes to date, does it not? If you should be considering talking dirty, you are probably dreaming about something a little more bothersome compared to that. However, before we proceed in that, still another thing to consider: the very most effective dirty talk is composed of words which create pictures in mind. The finest dirty-talk needs to paint an image of closeness and heat, the one which feeds his every appetite and produces a living, breathing film directly in the front of him. Every single word of your cluttered talk needs to create those pictures and put you directly in the center of those. You wish to be not merely in his bed, however in his mind too. Start by becoming familiar with your noises and your own emphasis. Then you are all set to start becoming familiar with the intense dirty-talk that you both may cherish.

How can I make it?

If you are reading this, you are on the ideal path to becoming familiar with all those naughty words. Learning is your ideal method to overcome your anxieties, and also this publication is supposed to assist you to do so. Additionally, it is a fantastic bet you are already believing a cluttered thought or 2 as you see, which is fine -- since it starts on your thoughts. Actually, let us start at this time.

Take some time to consider these questions:

What's the strangest thing you can see right now?

If you think about your spouse, what is the one thing concerning him that turns you more than whatever else?

Consider the last time you had intercourse -- that which was that the only thing that he'd you enjoyed the most?

What exactly did you do if he did this?

Can you inform him with phrases with noises, or together with all the motion of your entire body, just how much you adored?

How can he respond?

Consider the sensual activity. What do you adore most about gender with your spouse?

Picture his entire body. What would you like about doing it? What type of sounds does he create?

Which sound or word out of him turns on more compared to the others?

Now you are aware there are particular matters he enjoys -- what exactly are they all? Imagine them at the vivid, stunning, heart-pounding detail you'll be able to muster.

Are you really currently feeling sexy? If you're, and you're so inclined to go farther with all those notions in mind, now's that moment! Masturbation is just a fantastic means to master exactly what you would like. Now's a fantastic time to understand just what words direct you and the way to chat about what exactly is happening if you are all riled up. Locate time to creep into bed and start to play with, doing all of the items you might generally do only that moment, talk to it. Say what outloud. Nobody is about to know you, who cares in the event that you sound corny? Describe what you're doing. If you stroke your legs with your palms, say. Should you rub your breasts with the fingers, say, too. Are your nipples hard? Say it out loud. Play different words for human body parts. Touch name and yourself exactly what you're touching. This really is a great time to discover which words feel taboo. Can the phrase "cunt" irritate you? Is it true that the phrase "pussy" looks like a superior fit? That will be a lot easier to say? What type turns you? What type turns off you? In case you have never mentioned those words earlier, take action today, and continue doing this before you decide the way you are feeling about them. How do you feel if your spouse used these same words? Close your eyes and imagine it. How do you respond? Picture your partner saying those words in your ear. How does the system respond? Find what turns you say it, repeatedly. Becoming comfy with expression this is part of this conflict. You have got to prepare yourself to state it to a spouse, also. Focused on the way you may appear or seem for those who start into your filthy talk? Start with looking to a mirror and talking about your own. Give yourself a sexy appearance at the same time you state just how much you really enjoy having your breasts. Blow a kiss. Discuss how it makes your pussy tingle if he does this certain thing, which drives you crazy. Are you laughing yet? Good! Obtain the giggles out today, while it's only you and the chick from the mirror. Get as absurd as gloomy as you would like! In reality, make an effort to make yourself laugh. The best way crazy is it possible to receive? Just how much on the edge of how "available" is it possible to go? Enjoy it! Now it may appear that speaking filthy with no discussion is hopeless; however, the further you work on saying those words which produce you blush, the easier it is going to purchase. Doing something is tough; nevertheless, after performing this fifty times, unexpectedly, it sounds easier. Some individuals are concerned with the direction they'll seem if they decide to try to talk dirty. If you are focused on the way, your voice will seem once you are stressed and hot, spend money on a cassette recorder, or make use of the voice memo work onto your own mobile to record yourself as you masturbate. Bear in mind, nobody will hear it you personally, and also, you'll be able to disable it instantly after you tune in. Should you decide to perform this, pay attention to your voice changes since you become turned on. That hot breathlessness on your voice is what's going to make your partner moving! Say anything concerns mind because you do so, including filthy words. Get creative! If you play with back the tape, consider just how sexy you seem -- and also make a note of words that sound particularly beautiful once they originate in the trembling lips. Understand what we mentioned before: performing this is tough; however, the longer you can do it, the simpler it gets. Practice, practice, and also much more exercise makes perfect!

Chapter three

Fine-tuning your bedroom talk

You've built intimacy outside the bedroom, and you've made your thoughts on dirty talk very clear by now. You've gotten creative with love notes, and you've made some sexy phone calls. You've both been swept away by the teasing and innuendo from time to time, and now you are both walking with a little bounce in your step. You've even tried reading erotica to him, and succeeded in getting you both turned on with the words. But those were someone else's words. Now it's time to start creating your own. Don't know where to begin? You're not alone. But by this point, you should have a pretty good idea of what works for your partner. Better yet, you have a good idea of what works for you. You know what turns you on, and you know what works for both of you. Keep that in mind as you decide what you're going to say to your partner to break that dirty talk ice. Start with descriptions of his body. Remember, it doesn't have to be hard-core! Here are a few suggestions on where to begin: tell him how strong he is. Tell him how much it turns you on when you look at his muscular arms, or his trim waist, or his long, sexy legs. Does he have a hairy chest? Tell him how much you like to tangle your fingers in it. Does he have long hair? Tell him how much you love to watch it fall around his face when he makes love to you. Does he have broad shoulders? Describe how it feels to hold onto them while he's moving above you, how he makes you feel safe and secure, or how his size makes you feel submissive. Tell him about looking down at him when you're on top, and how much you love to see the pleasure in his eyes. You should have no problem finding those things you love about your lover's body. There's a reason you love to go to bed with him, and a reason you want to make your sex life even hotter -- you've got one hell of a guy! So tell him that, and everything else that comes to mind about how wonderful he is. Get a little more explicit as things heat up. Now is when you can point out more intimate things about him, and use them to fuel your dirty talk. Here are a few more explicit suggestions: tell him how much you love to feel him inside you. Moan about how thick he is, or how long, or how he fits you just right. Tell him how much you love it when he works magic with his fingers – between your legs, over your nipples, anywhere on your body. Tell him how hard your nipples are. Ask him if he can feel how wet you are. Remind him that he's the one you've been fantasizing about all day. Ask him to talk to you, too. What does he like to feel when he's in bed with you? What is his favorite position? What does he like to see you do? What is his ultimate fantasy? What was his favorite moment out of all the times you have made love? What made it so special? Prompt him a bit if he's shy, and he will start to reciprocate with his own thoughts. If he's really into talking dirty with you by now, this is when things could start to get a bit more hard-core. What fun! Here are a few questions to get you started. Whisper them into his ear at the appropriate time and let nature take its course: do you like it when I get on top? Do you ever think about being tied up? Would you rather do it with the lights on or off? Tell me why you like it that way. What's the one thing we've never tried that you really want to do? What do you want me to do? What's your favorite thing to do to me? When do you come harder? When you're standing up, or sitting up, or lying down? Do you like it when I do this? What do you want me to wear tonight? Another surefire way to start the dirty talk is to describe what he's doing to you. If he slips his hand between your legs, that's a good time to whisper how much you like it. "I love it when you touch me there" is good, but "I love it when you touch my pussy" might be better. Gauge his reactions to your words, and adjust them accordingly. If "pussy" turns him on and you're not opposed to the sound of it, try using "cunt" instead. If that gets him going, use it again, only with more emphasis. Now is the time to use your new vocabulary! Add a bit more. Perhaps he loves to hear the word "cunt," and maybe you like it, too. So try something to describe it a bit more. "tight cunt" or "wet cunt" or "slippery cunt" might be good things to try. Then put it into a sentence. "I love it when you touch my hot, wet cunt." describe what you're doing to him, too. Remember, creating images is what dirty talk does best, and you want him to see the fantasy before you make it a reality. "I'm going to taste you" is a good way to let him know you're going to perform oral. "I'm going to go down on you" is better. "I'm going to suck your cock" is even better than that. Is he hard? Is he throbbing? "I'm going to suck your hard, throbbing cock" is the blunt, honest truth. Then do it! The fantasy is already in his head, and feeling you do exactly what you said you would be going to be a huge turn-on. Besides that, the next time you talk dirty to him, he will remember that you did exactly what you said you would -- and that will fuel his fantasies the next time you're talking to him with that naughty mouth of yours. Most of all, be confident. You already know he likes it when you do certain things. Maybe he loves the way you go down on him. You don't have to ask him if he likes it – you already know he does. "you like the way I suck your dick, don't you?" It can be a taunting challenge. "yeah, I know you like that." What other things might you say to turn him on even more?

Taking it further: phone sex

If you have ever been in a situation where your lover was a thousand miles away from you -- or even just down the street -- and you were too horny to think straight, you can grasp the appeal of phone sex. Having sex on the phone is the original form of dirty talk! People have been having phone sex for as long as the phone has existed. In the early days, when phone lines were called "party lines," and several people could listen in at once, it was probably a bit daunting to attempt phone sex. But you can bet someone, at some point, gave it a shot -- and you can bet that was one blushing operator who had the pleasure of listening in! Flash forward to around 1980, when someone realized they could make money through phone sex. The first phone sex hotlines went live. All it took was a phone call, and a credit card number and phone sex was yours for the taking. In the late one980s, the 900-number was introduced, and phone sex became a quite popular hobby for some. With 900 numbers, it was easier than ever to explore fetishes or find the kind of dirty talk you desired, all with the simple touch of a button. The phone sex industry did a booming business, and continues to do so today, despite the advent of the internet and free calling plans to virtually anywhere in the world. Now that phone sex has become more mainstream and accepted, the thought of someone having it isn't as shocking as it once was. Phone sex used to be something shameful, a kind of sex that was paid for, only one step above prostitution. When it was used in conjunction with a long-distance relationship, it was kept very quiet, in hopes of not sullying the reputations of those who had given in to their desires. But now that long-distance relationships are fostered by the internet and travel for business has become almost the norm, phone sex has become an accepted and even expected act for those who cannot be together in the physical sense. Have you ever tried phone sex? If you haven't, now is the time! As we said earlier, phone sex is the original form of dirty talk. You can't use the motion of your body to seduce your lover, and you can't give them pleasure by touching them. All you have are your words and those delicious sounds that come when you're turned on. But when it comes to phone sex, that is more than enough to make it work for both of you. Don't know how to get started? Many people don't. You might think the idea of phone sex is all well and good, but when you do get your partner on the phone, you might be so tonguetied that you can't think of what to say, much less how to say it. Here are a few tips to make those first moments easier. After that, things should just happen naturally. Get started before you call. Look at porn, read erotica, play with your vibrator -- do whatever you usually do to get all hot and bothered when you are alone. When you are on the edge of breathless, pick up the phone. Choose your time. If you really want phone sex but you know your partner is in a meeting and they simply cannot get out, you might be out of luck at the moment. Try to plan your phone sex for a time when you know your lover will be alone, or at least in a place where they can listen to you without being interrupted. Set the mood. Phone sex is a very real kind of sex. So prepare for it just as you would prepare to meet your lover at the door! Wear the sexiest lingerie, something that makes you feel like a queen. Light a candle, turn down the covers and have your sexy toys ready to help you out. Charge it up. It might sound like a very simple thing, but it's important. Charge your phone before you make that call! There is nothing more frustrating than being right on the edge of a good orgasm and hearing that annoying "low battery" beep. While you're at it, turn off your call waiting. That's a beeping sound you don't want to hear either! Be ready to give. What if you call your partner while they are sitting in traffic? They might not be able to participate physically, but they can certainly listen to you as you do your thing...you naughty, naughty dirty talker! Speak in a low, sultry growl. Your voice can sound even sexier on the phone than it does in person! If you pitch your voice a bit lower, you will sound more seductive, and your phone sex partner will eat it up. Push his hot buttons. You know what turns your lover on, so capitalize on it. Now is the time to spin a fantasy that will paint a vivid picture in their head. Talk your way through it, from the opening tease to the closing climax. Tell him what to do. Phone sex can be a great time to order your partner around, and who doesn't love having the pressure off for a while? All your lover has to do is follow your suggestions until they get off. Very few things beat the feeling of that, don't you think? Get hardcore. Crude, raunchy words are the best when it comes to phone sex. If you are the shy type, it might seem as though you can't get past that barrier that keeps you tongue-tied, but phone sex might surprise you. Get your own. Phone sex is about sharing fantasies and getting off to them -- but it doesn't mean it's all about him. It can be all about you, too! Touch yourself while you talk dirty to your partner over the phone. Let yourself come -- and let your partner hear it. There are few things sexier than the sound of someone reaching the ultimate pleasure, and your lover will be happy to share that moment with you. Phone sex is great for those who feel a bit inhibited about their dirty talk. If you aren't quite ready to try it in a face-to-face situation, phone sex gives you the perfect opportunity. If you get uncomfortable, you can stop the phone sex abruptly, and you don't have to be bashful about it. If you want to try out something extra raunchy, you can do it without letting your lover see you blush and tremble. If you need to ease into things, phone sex offers a level of comfort that you can't find when the barriers are down, and that person is standing right in front of you. Those who are in long-distance relationships, and especially those who have phone sex before they met in person often have a much easier time with getting their sex life in tune with one another. Why? They have already touched on the intimacy that phone sex provides. They already know what turns the other person on, and they have had time to explore fantasies, dreams, and desires through a non-threatening medium. For those who are able to see each other every day, phone sex adds a new dimension to their lovemaking. The tease can be drawn out over the span of the entire day, not just from the moment he walks in the door after a hard day at work. A quickie during the noon hour, with the door closed and locked, makes phone sex quite an appealing option for both of you! When you think of phone sex, you probably think of having your partner on the phone with you while you are doing naughty things and spinning those fantasy tales, but there are a few other dimensions to phone sex you might want to consider. If you call and your partner doesn't answer the phone, what do you do? You leave a dirty message! It can be something very simple, just a basic "I want you now" kind of tone, one that will get his attention and make him smile. Or it could be something much more raunchy. If you're really brave, you could masturbate to the point of orgasm, and then call your partner and leave the sounds of your climax on voicemail. It helps if you have an idea of how long the voicemail will record -- some will handle only thirty seconds, while others handle up to five minutes or even more, depending upon their phone service. Be sure to end the call with a giggle and a kiss before hanging up the phone. But talking on the phone is not the only form of phone sex. There is another, more modern form...and it's not just for teenagers anymore!

Make it quick! Dirty texting

Don't have the time or the inclination to talk on the phone when you're feeling naughty? Dirty texting is all the rage, and for a good reason. Dirty texting can be done anywhere, anytime, without much risk of anyone finding out what you are doing. Certainly, no one can overhear you when you're texting! Also known as "sexting" (a combination of the words "sex" and "text"), the trend toward using phone text to get naughty with your partner started many years ago. Teenagers were the first to realize they could send naughty text messages, and as long as they kept their phone private or deleted the messages when they were done, no one was the wiser. After all, most phone services do track how many text messages you send, but they don't track what you say! But now the trend has widened to include everyone, even older adults. According to a recent study by the aarp, baby boomers love technology - - and they are taking advantage of sexting simply because it's downright fun. And of course, most cell phones these days have the ability for texting, so it's very simple for anyone to do. But where do you begin? Sexting might be catching on like wildfire, but for those who haven't dealt with it before, knowing what to say and how to say it can be rather daunting. Here are a few tips: start out very simple. In fact, start out with basic conversation. Ask how their day was. Tell them you are thinking about them. Ask what they might like to do when you are together again. Tell them that you want them. Anything short and sweet, something to break the ice and become a bit more intimate. When you have warmed up to texting with your partner, get a bit more suggestive. "I can't wait to see you" is a good one, and so is "I miss having you in our bed." gauge the response you get by how enthusiastic it seems. If they respond in kind, you're being invited -- and even encouraged! - - to keep the conversation moving into the more naughty territory. Keep the text short. You probably have a lot to say, but you don't have much room in which to say it. The shorter your texts are, the less time you spend typing -- and that means you hit the send button faster. The texts show up on your partner's phone at regular intervals, instead of with long pauses between each one. This helps keep the fire hot, especially when you're in the middle of a good fantasy. If they ask for more, start telling them about your latest fantasy. Start out easy, with soft and tender words, then move into the raunchier set when it is clear your partner is wanting something more. Want to spice things up and simply surprise your partner into a smile? Send a raunchy text right off the bat. This is especially effective if you are the shy type and have trouble easing into dirty talk with your lover. They will be very pleasantly surprised by your naughty foray into the texting world! When you are in the mood to dirty text messages to your partner, don't hesitate to use the common texting abbreviations, such as "u" for you or "c" for see. This will make things go faster, and the dirty talk will have the same effect! If you want to spice up the dirty texting even further, you can always send photos of yourself, taken with your phone. Simply use the camera, then click on the options feature and hit "send." be sure you are sending the photograph to the right person, and be sure this is a person you can trust. Often explicit photos wind up being passed around or shared with friends, and might even wind up on the internet, where anyone can see you in a compromising position. So have fun, but be careful! Keep in mind a bit of housekeeping, however. Remember that when you receive or send a text, it is saved on your phone. If your phone is used by someone else, even in the most innocent manner, they might hit a button that allows them to see your photos or text messages. If this is a concern for you, be sure to delete the messages and photos you have sent and received. If you want to save them, look into how you can download information from your phone to your computer and put them on a disk or your hard drive before you delete them. Clearing out your texts and pictures periodically is a good idea anyway. If you lost your phone and it was found by an unscrupulous character, all of your information could wind up on the internet -- or those naughty pictures could be sent to every person in your address book. It sounds like a nightmare, but it has happened before, and it will probably happen again. Just don't let it happen to you! Now that the housekeeping is out of the way to start planning your first dirty talk text! What will you say? How will you say it? What fantasy will you spin for your partner? Sometimes the anticipation and planning is just as good as the sexting itself!

Playing online: cybersex and email

Phone sex and texting are not the only routes to a good dirty talk time. Have you ever teased your partner through a naughty email flirtation? Email messages back and forth can spin a tale that lasts for months. Email forces you to slow down and take your time in writing what you want to say. Much like writing a love letter with pen and paper, email is the slower version of the texting craze... and it can be just as powerful. When you are talking dirty through email, it's best to take it slow at first and test the waters. Your email partner might be at work, or in a situation where naughty emails could be intercepted by someone who shouldn't see them. In that case, taking it slow is the prudent way to go. Trust your partner to lead you into the dirty talk themselves. If they want more, they can invite you to say more. If they tell you they are the only one who reads that email account, for instance, you know that you can say whatever you like! If you are talking to your partner and you know you're dealing with a work email, maybe you can get away with a tease or two, but little more than that. It all depends on the situation, but you should always be certain of the situation before you jump into the naughtiest bits! Once you know the situation, let your dirty talk begin! Sexy emails are a great way to liven up the day and keep your partner thinking about you while he's away. You can start very simply and remind them of what you did together last night. Or you can talk about anticipation, and say that you can't wait until they get back so you can do it all again! If you want to go further, consider writing an erotic story in a series of emails. You can make it all about your partner. Create a fantasy about the two of you and weave it together with dirty words, then send the email and wait for a response. If your response is "give me more," then you're in luck. If the response is another part of your erotic story, one that your partner has written, then you're in even better luck! Writing an erotic story back and forth is one of the hottest ways to get sexy emails moving. If you want to add some spice to your emails, attach pictures of yourself doing naughty things. Or simply send an email that says, "can you guess what I'm doing right now?" and then launch into a vivid description of what your partner would see if they were there with you. Another popular form of dirty talk happens over instant messenger services or in chat rooms. "cybersex," sometimes simply known as "cyber," is a great way to talk to someone over the computer when you're in the mood for something naughty. Instant messenger services bring the power of dirty talk right to your fingertips -- literally! -- and allow you to form a bit of a deeper bond than that of a chat room flirtation. This is an excellent way to try out your new dirty talk and see the kind of reaction you get. It works especially well if you have a particular fetish or fantasy that you might be worried about sharing with a partner. Consider it a test drive! The anonymity of chat rooms makes it easy to put your thoughts and feelings out there and get an honest response in return. After all, you don't know these people, and they don't know you. If you say something that shocks them, they can tell you without fear of hurting your feelings, or vice versa. Whether you are playing with cybersex in a chat room or on your instant messenger program, there are a few rules of etiquette that apply: just watch at first. When you first enter a chat room, it might be tempting to jump into the fray. Resist the urge! Watch for a while. Eventually, you will see someone whose comments are witty enough or interesting enough to keep your attention. Then you can jump in and make comments in the current conversation that are directed toward that person. Or you can go the more direct route and ask to speak to them privately. Sexy chats might happen in open chat rooms, but if you want to get to the serious action, take it private. Ask the person you are interested in if they would like to embark on a private chat. Then you can see where that cyber road leads! Don't push for any information at all. Age, sex, and location are the basics that most people ask for in a chat room. Be honest about your sex -- are you male or female? You can be vague about your age and your location unless you are looking to take your cyber chats to "real life" at some point in the future. If you're just playing and brushing up on your dirty talk, you needn't bother with specifics. Keep in mind that the person you are talking to doesn't owe you any details, either, so don't ask for them. When you get into dirty talk in your chats, keep in mind the same rules as with texting. Keep the messages short and sweet in order to keep them coming quickly. You are essentially writing an erotic story in one-line increments, so keep in mind the flow of the action. You want to build up to a crescendo! Don't come and run. If you are so turned on by the dirty talk on the screen that your body simply can't hold back, good for you! But don't get yours and then call it a night. There is someone at the other end of that modem, and they are waiting for the same courtesy. On the other hand, if you are worried that the person you are cybering with will decide to cut and run themselves, get yours first! Talk through the session with them, and encourage them to respond to you, instead of just spinning your tale and helping them get off. The best cyber sessions are those when you are both participating, and you both get off at about the same time. When the cyber session is over, remember to thank them for a great time. If you are on instant messenger, it's possible you could talk to them again, so say goodbye with grace. If you are in a chat room and completely anonymous, say goodnight before you log off anyway -- it's just the polite thing to do. And of course, if you were having a cyber session with your lover while they were far away from you, blow them a virtual kiss and tell them that you can't wait until they get home, so you can whisper all that dirty talk right into their ear -- and then follow up on your naughty promises!

Chapter four

Dirty talk in public

Phone texting, sex, cybersex, email... All of these are things that maintain the filthy conversation between you and your partner. However, how about this exhibitionist side of you personally, the one which cries how poorly you need your partner, plus it is irrelevant where? You might maintain a public park, a railway station, a discount store, the financial institution, and even in the household. Maybe you've had a lot of at the Xmas party, or maybe you are all set to receive it on at the pool. In any case, might be, you are able to talk dirty -- and you are in public areas. Not a problem! The best technique for talking dirty in people is to make certain nobody knows precisely what you're saying. They may imagine, convinced, but who cares? Should they don't really understand without a doubt, they can not call you on it! When you can manage to receive your partner sexy and sexy as you're in a public atmosphere, you are certain to get some wonderful actions whenever you do arrive at a relaxing and private place. Below are a couple strategies to begin talking dirty in people: whisper it. The very populous, crazy dirty-talk is stated using a whisper. Say it with a sly grin and let your lips brush the fan's ear since you let them know exactly what you desire to complete in their mind later. Or that which you need them to complete for your requirements. Actually, when it's a quick and pleasant opinion, something such as"I need to fuck you," it's sufficient to have the ball rolling. Show it. Say it along with your own eyes. Let your partner know you just want them by how you glance at them. Good dirty-talk may comprise more than simply words! Make a place of appearing in the lover's tight, sexy cute butt with pride in your eyes. Make certain that you get stuck doing this! If you would like to get right to the purpose, shed your own eyes into his crotch, linger there some time, then look back into your own eyes. Any man worth his salt will soon know exactly what that look means! Slip a way. Simply take the opportunity for you to hide out for some time and enjoy a small amount of appetite. Perhaps it is possible to discover a secluded hallway and cop a feel. Maybe you are able to sneak a profound French kiss as you're headed to the kitchen to match your beverage. Whenever you do slide away, be sure that you set your feelings into words. Cause them to become clear and to the purpose. "I want to suck you off to the table" can be just a fantastic way to elevate your buff's eyebrows! Let the body do the talking. Whenever you are standing close, brush your breasts against his spine. Let your buttocks touch. Put your arm. Slip down your hand to an improper place today and then, however, just for an instant, before anybody else could grab onto exactly what that gloomy hand is doing. Lean over and utilize the dirty words to finish the emotional picture. Innuendo galore! Certainly, one of the coolest things about a filthy conversation in people is that moment when someone says something totally innocent...nevertheless, you hear it within a totally naughty method. Dirty thoughts build, one after another. The further cluttered your thinking will be, the more inclined you should observe the many naive comments as raunchy chances. As an example, if someone expresses it's hot out, you could lean to a partner and say, "maybe not as sexy as it will be " the dual significance won't be lost to these, and so on you'll be laughing in the most useful "naive" opinions -- and becoming switched at exactly the exact same moment. Make dirty conversation in people a match the 2 of you play with together. Inform your spouse at the onset of the evening which you're going to undoubtedly be talking dirty to him that the whole time, and have him to rely on the number of dirty-talk opinions they will capture. Subsequently, slide into those naughty innuendos every chance you will get! Below are a couple of suggestions to help get this gloomy innuendo started: while at a fourth of July party, speak to just how nicely those temples are "shooting" to the atmosphere. Tell him just how much you really want the noise of this "cannon" and inquire whether he believes they have been planning to "blow" a whole lot larger for the "orgasm" when at the shore, say that cream feels "thick and warm and creamy" like something you may think about...when you visit someone about the surfboard, mention that you'll really like to become riding something hard, too. Maybe the very thought of this something hard it which makes you wet as a sea! At a friend's party? Discuss the way you adore the taste of the jello "shooters" and point out that the restroom is far a lot more than big enough for just two. If you should be in an incredibly adventuresome mood and you also understand that your partner is a thing a little more "enjoyable," play with a match of speaking about that man at your buddy's party are the loudest in bed, or that you would love to invitation for a threesome. Discussing of threesomes and other naughty tid-bits

People "whoa!" seconds

We've mentioned how dirty-talk creates pictures in mind, images that function to direct your spouse. Speaking about what you are doing during intercourse, or requesting him exactly what he wants one to accomplish, opens the doorway to deeper conversation. People do a good deal of things from the heat of fire they mightn't ordinarily do, and you should immediately realize they say things that they normally wouldn't state, too. One dream contributes into still another, yet still another, and so on, you may end up exploring land you won't ever have differently, had you never heard that this fresh foul speech. Opinions may be earned in the heat of fire that surprises you, make you uneasy, as well as shock you. You could hear matters you had never anticipated, and you also could not understand just how to react. However, before you become angry, look at this: whenever you are switched on beyond belief, how have you been thinking about that which is from the mouthwatering? Are you aware of the small pops and sighs you simply can't appear to help? It's exactly the same with a vibrant dream -- whether or not it's on mind, it's probably likely to be said at a certain time, however raunchy or taboo it's. That is one of those cool ideas about mindblowing gender: it completely destroys the filter that typically governs the mouth area! If a partner does feel liberated to express what for you, which you've never heard previously, make an effort to contain your shock in what's said. Remember: you are hearing these matters as you've accumulated the closeness between both of you personally, and discussing those dreams requires an enormous step of confidence. When he did not hope you, then you'll not be hearing his innermost thoughts and secrets! The simple fact he has only told you something really intimate about his wants speaks volumes regarding the way he feels about you personally. Therefore be thankful he is able to say such things! Granted, a number of dreams might be gasp-inducing. It may be something as straightforward as requesting to wear high heeled boots and fishnets at bed; also, it may possibly be something as jaw-dropping as though he'd really like to see one with the other woman -- or even some other guy! The graphics that your good dirty conversation paints within his mind could swell into pictures which you never imagined are there. This is actually a standard development, although you could be taken aback in the beginning, it's essential to not forget this heightened familiarity is a fantastic thing. Try to not get confused by the dreams he relates, however, do not accept these since the gospel, either. Studies indicate that ninety percent of dreams are simply that -- dream. They're matters which turn you when you consider these; however, you may not perform in actuality, given that the ability. Lots of men and women discuss exactly what they'd really like to complete, or they could take to one afternoon, however, few really chase it. The dream is normally enough. Sharing those dreams may cause amazing sex between the 2 of you; however, it generally does not suggest he wishes to own this wonderful sex using four or three -- or even longer! If you are into a dirty conversation, then you are already pretty openminded. Keep this receptive mind once you are at the heat of the fire and talking dreams. Who knows? You may possibly get in the scenario and also be turned, it will become a dream of yours too! However, if the bedroom matches are over and it's really only the couple at the afterglow, you could begin to wonder about what that came from the mouth area. Can he really mention just how good it is to see with another guy? Can he be really to with two ladies during sex together with him? And lord have mercy, did he really mean it if he said he wished to stop by a gay strip club? You might discover some crazy objects once the inhibitions are unleashed. Below are a few chances. How do you believe if you hear a couple of these? I would like to see you during sex with another guy. I would like to see you during sex with another lady. I would like to let my very best friend take a look. I would like one to complete me as if my cousin did me personally. I'd like being tied up and spanked. I would like one to visit a strip club and see you get yourself a lap dancing. I would like one to see me have a lap dancing. I would like to try out smoking buds while we put it all on. I would like you to whip me. I would like to meet with a stranger in a hotel room and have sex. I would like to dress up in your clothes. I would like to test out women and also men. I would like to get fucked up the bum with a strap on. I'd like to inform you and cause you to call me daddy. I would like one to bark like a dog while I fuck you. I would like to find out you decorate in leather. (or perhaps just a french maid outfit, or hooker heels, etc.) That I need to make you my sex slave. Therefore...what exactly do you really think? Do some of these tricks allow you to cringe? Do someone of these turn you? Can a number of them cause you to desire to quit reading? All these are now pretty tame when compared with this huge dream worlds within our minds. Your man may have a really special fantasy that has quite a while to spell out. Or it may be something you've never been aware of earlier. Again, do not judge this, and do not make an effort to show off him from that which he is simply told you. Bear in mind the dilemma of trust, and also just how much it required him to express the things for you. Think of it as a compliment! Bear in mind: your partner probably needed a sexual past until you came across, and you also have been round the block several times, too. In any event, because he says it can't mean he wishes to accomplish it, and only because he said it can't mean he has been down the road. It's possible to take those dreams for what they have been -- a filthy conversation between two different people at a fervent moment -- or you'll be able to ask additional questions. However, before you do this, bear in mind that your fantasies. What are you ever said in the heat of fire which you'll not truly do? Research indicates that lots of women think of being accepted by greater than one person, but the majority of them could not actually decide to try it.

Research also demonstrates that rape is now an interest of many women's dreams, but not one of these would really want it to manifest! What happens within our own minds, in our private thoughts, is frequently not something which meshes together with this true to life. This is exactly why it's referred to as a dream. If you're still determined to arrive at the underside of the dreams, be warned: don't ask if that you never desire to understand! If you'd rather never to be worried about your partner's sexual history, do not inquire if certain dreams really happened. He would let you know that the reality, of course, should you've got any jealousy in any way, you may possibly turn green with jealousy and crimson with anger. He may possibly lie for you personally, which divides the closeness you've assembled, and that makes him likely to maintain his head to himself on out. However, if you should be entirely confident in your relationship and prepared to be adventurous because he's, by all means, talk every dream that springs to mind.

There is nothing sexier than understanding what a sexual encounter your partner needs, and establishing that do or may result in some intense debate -- and who knows? Some particular "whoa" moments only may result in some intense experiences you never dreamed you'd pursue!

Naughty role playing strategies and tricks

The area of role-playing could be the basis of a filthy conversation. Discussing filthy can indicate telling a narrative for the own lover, slowly offering a dream in words, the one which is going to turn them by the graphics you paint within the mind. Role-playing takes this idea a step farther and turns out that dream in reality -- as close to reality as it could possibly capture. By now, you're well in the sphere of dirty talk, along with your buff has probably shared with a thing or 2 about his dreams as well as exactly what he'd really like to do, even if the chance ever arose. If those dreams direct you too, you can think about making them a real possibility with role playing. Some dreams are so prevalent there are whole guide-books, theatres, and also communities specializing in the quest for those. Some of those role-playing towns and activities may possibly be far from your own safe place, or maybe you discover that something that you never thought would attract you actually causes you to feel quite comfortable.

That is among the greatest reasons for having self-indulgent: that you have no idea whether you enjoy it before you decide to try it, but should you enjoy it, then you still want it a long time! Below are a number of naughty role playing scenarios. Has your spouse spoken about every one of them? Does someone of them light the flame for you personally? A stern headmaster is seduced by a student. A man becomes deflowered by means of a prostitute. An avid piano teacher simplifies a pupil for practicing. A pirate kidnaps a reasonable maiden, and it has his way with her. The poor boy that was only discharged from prison finds himself drawn to his parole officer. The inmate from the prison has an affair with a warden. A married woman matches somebody else to get gender at a hotel. A joyful mother has sex with Santa Claus. A physician has his manner with an individual. The naughty nurse extends above and beyond the call of responsibility. The fitness expert has in certain overtime. The mechanic and also the woman in misery work-out an exceptional kind of payment.

Assembling a stranger across the net turns in to a public sexual encounter. An unscrupulous manager blackmails a porn celebrity for favors. A female is passed around between half a dozen men. A guy is tied to the bed and made to execute for a variety of ladies. A trainer instructs his"pony" just how to do because of him personally. Two unidentified strangers speak or view one another's faces; however, they will have a gloomy anal session whenever they have been together. The maid supplies services to this individual of the home. The campground takes good care of a lot more than only the babysitting. The librarian uniquely hushes the loud patron. The role of playing some ideas can be utterly infinite. Even within a definite dream, there might be heaps of variations, all these worth an attempt for the role-playing hall of fame. You are able to try out every role-playing scenario you can imagine, but not scratch the face of everything can be potential! However, to start your venture to role-playing, choose something easy todo. Something it does not require many props is obviously a fantastic bet. If you're playing the librarian and patron, a very simple suit and also a couple of glasses, together with your own hair pulled up into a bun, will suit just fine. You ought to have a bookshelf nearby, full of novels, and a good deal of opportunity to generate noise in a quiet room. It's also advisable to possess a severe attitude to cooperate side the librarian motif. If you're increasingly anonymous strangers, then the largest challenge is finding a solution to stay "anonymous" while making love. Perhaps you feign to generally meet at a hotel room after getting hired around the web? An individual might possibly be looking forward to one other, and also the actions could happen doggie style. However, naturally, that's just one small thought out from the heaps you can actually decide to try! Look online or in a masturbator shop to detect the appropriate role-playing clothes if your situation demands it. A french maid costume is not difficult to get; therefore, it is just a pirate. The others may be much more difficult or expensive. If you're playing a stripper, then you may like to decide on the conventional stripper heels along with also the rod, needless to say -- and also those matters may take the money and time. All of it is dependent on how much you truly would like to decide on your role-playing games. As important because the outfits and mindset are your dirty-talk! Tailor your cluttered speak to match the specific situation you're portraying. As an example, a librarian could be correct before the fire took more, then her mouth may possibly be filthy as this of a sailor. The captive could be gloomy, whilst the warden would make an effort to find matters more diplomatically, as well as possibly even mete out a punishment when a curse-word were used. On occasion, the finest dirty-talk has become easily the most restricted, as when it comes to this headmaster and student -- you really need to find very creative once the foul conversation wouldn't match the funniest game! In cases like this, you're able to consider punishments for discussing dirty, which may serve to reevaluate the specific situation more. On occasion, a very simple role playing game can become a comprehensive way of life. For anyone that likes bondage or entry, their very first forays into role playing may possibly have become the catalyst, which led them to pick out a full-time way of life. You never understand what role-playing may perform; nevertheless, you do understand it may result in a more romantic and more enjoyable relationship while in the bedroom. And that does not desire to really have the most interesting potential behind-closed-doors?

Girl on girl dirty-talk

During this publication, we've talked a little about the dirty conversation to somebody, and our opinions are aimed toward "him"; however, think about the "her" side of this equation? If a woman talks dirty to some other woman, can it be any different than if a woman talks dirty to a guy? The reply to this is yes...no. There appears to be an enormous misconception boating about filthy and women talk. Therefore oftentimes, women are considered to be the delicate blossom, the one which really should not be sullied by filthy items. Including sexual dreams, colorful sexual saying, and even down and dirty gloomy conversation. It harkens back to a period when women were regarded as the weaker gender, and so were believed to want protection from many matters which may"tainted" their tender and unassuming character. How My times have changed! Women are extremely responsible for their lifestyles. Women's joy of pornography, dirty conversation, and also other items considered overly"base" for its normal woman has gotten more conventional and accepted in the last several decades. The sexual revolution demonstrated to women they could have sexual dreams and dreams which were equally strong -- maybe even much more! -- compared to that of the male counterparts. Functioning on this sexual side is now more prevalent, now women are permitted to take care of their particular bodies also search their own joy. They would like to listen to those words that are naughty! Many folks still prefer to express dirty talk is demeaning for women, and they ought to just hear the many tender and adoring words out of their partner. This stems from precisely the exact same mindset, which says women should just have sex for procreation and may not see pornography. Inside this sort of mindset, there's not any space for your own lesbian woman along with the homosexual individual. The idea wouldn't cross their heads! Dirty talk isn't demeaning. It's not demeaning if a woman says it into still another, and it's not exactly when a gentleman says, either.

In reality, it's just the contrary -- it's enabling. Dirty conversation is a method of opening to joy and demonstrating dozens of stereotypes wrong! It's really a method of requesting exactly what you would like and with every anticipation to setting it up. Dirty conversation opens the doors of sexual relationship between two different people, also permits them to go ahead to a meaningful, enlightening relationship. Once you talk dirty to one another, you're learning increasingly more with every breath. What relationship wouldn't gain out of this? In terms of technique in regards to girl on girl dirty discussion, it comes right down to doing everything seems good, and loving every single minute of this. Girl on girl dirty-talk may be the type of thing men dream of watching porn films, plus so they will have a valid reason -- filthy conversation, no matter who's receiving and giving, is among the latest things around. One of the proposals in this publication might be tailored to exactly the exact same-gender relationship. When it is a person speaking with another guy or some woman seeking to find still another woman sexy, all of exactly the very same rules apply. Never forget to take care of your partner with the most respect and courtesy, if or not described as a person or woman -- however, once the bedroom door shuts behind the both of you personally, absolutely anything goes wrong. Do not allow preconceived thoughts of "the stronger gender" or even," the weaker sex" enter the form of familiarity!

Use dirty talking to spice up your relationship

Dirty talking isn't necessarily an art people learn through the time of growing up as you've got to be around it to discover what it really is and also how it would always be to be properly used. I believe this can be the situation with talking filthy now. Lots of men and women on earth do not know the objective of this and misuse it to a degree at which it really should not be mistreated. If you did not understand already, filthy speaking cases are mostly utilized in relationships that are growing stronger daily. The cause for that is that talking dirty to a partner spices your relationship.

Currently, a great deal of people cannot know just how being uneasy by employing these examples is going to do some good in a connection, and that is since they grew up using it figured out just how to work with this procedure to be prosperous. Additionally, this is exactly why I stated it isn't an art, you know how to complete it you never. The men and women who do not understand just how exactly to do that the explicit talking utilization cases of filthy speaking for their partner that they find on internet sites, in novels, etc.. This way is nice and dandy too but once you find out the way the opposite sex really work learning the way to foul text on your own may drive your partner crazy.

Just how mad? They are always considering you through the entire afternoon, you will keep forever in your own mind. Your partner will soon have filthy ideas constantly within their mind. They'll take to and text you every chance they get simply to find out exactly what you need to state. They'll come home and need one so bad you'll almost have to beg them to not jump around you. Your partner may likewise be sending you dirty texting whenever they cannot locate a phone to call you. That is how mad dirty talking can, in fact, be if it's done correctly. I bet you'd be astonished if I let you know that studies with this sort of filthy conduct have been demonstrated to increase closeness amounts in relationships, boost lovemaking, improve confidence, and also the very astonishing one is that filthy speaking actually increases your odds of winning relationships. For a little time to consider any of it, it can seem sensible. The main reason relationships and unions arrive at an end are really because both or both spouses shed attention and begin cheating, but by keeping the magic living your becoming the partner totally hooked onto the excitement.

Learning how to talk dirty isn't too overly complicated. To start with, you've got to know how to become more familiar with what which are likely to be said. I advise a lot of people to go and hunt for dirty talking cases for men if you are a person and women to hunt for dirty discussing cases for ladies. This will provide you with an instant little heads up exactly what dirty talking happens to be. Only work on it slowly, and it is going to become increasingly more natural.

You've heard that old expression about having too much of a fantastic thing. Such a thing can be performed for excess - exercise, eating, shopping - also, heaven forbid, gender. That overpowering gender you'd the very first couple of days you spoke dirty made you realize everything you had was a fantastic thing, and you also have begun to experiment and longer, finding new paths to joy with the assistance of a couple of naughty words. But after tens of thousands of marathon sex sessions having dirty-talk involved with each of them, you could have begun to wonder how far is too far?

Make no mistake: dirty-talk will up the ante to get a few love life, and certainly will usually cause you and your fan closer together. The reciprocal joy of talking dirty, and also the data that is something only the both of you talk about, could cause you to really feel much closer for the person who you're sharing it with. Once you open about talking dirty in the bedroom, then this openness contributes to other communicating out the bedroom - not just does one talk more about gender and why is all you sign up, but talking results in a discussion of different facets of one's relationship. In a nutshell, talking dirty is excellent for you personally!

You understand you've got a touch a lot of dirty discussions the moment it starts to develop into a crutch to an emotional familiarity. In the event that you fail to get worked up in your partner without contemplating his dirty mouth, then it is the right time for you to pull a little and re think your sexual life. What could it be all about your partner who turns you - apart from words? What's all about him that made you need to be together with him at the first location? You required to research filthy conversation to boost your romantic relationship. But do not allow this foul conversation to become the cornerstone of what you do - it will not ever be the principal path, however, the spice which makes things interesting. If you feel you are talking dirty a touch too much, then consider moving straight back to the basic principles - no filthy conversation in any way. Only your breath, your organic noises that the fan attracts from you personally, and also the conversation of one's own bodies without words in any way. Is it just too arousing? Now you're an expert in dirty talk, gender without a voice may be more intriguing than ever you've spent some time communication in lots of ways, and eventually become close, that talking without words will soon come handy for you, and you'll certainly be thrilled with the brand new amount of familiarity.

Everywoman will admit this certain thing that's very critical in a relationship that must not be jeopardized is gender. Every person will acknowledge as long as their sexual lives are superb; they all have been prepared to do nearly anything to ensure the union or dating resides forever. The biggest hurdle, though gets reduce this monotony that accompany many relationships and unions throughout sexual activity. The solution for that really is quite simple actually: talking dirty during sexual activity. Even though dirty-talk is quite popular, perhaps not all girls know just how exactly to do it correctly. Most offer it a go one or two times, so when it will become embarrassing or awkward, provide up it.

I've a couple ideas which can allow you to realize what filthy speaking is and the way to accomplish it correctly. The very first trick I will offer you would be to seek out advice from the ideal sources. Don't listen to what your girlfriends state and follow along generously. There are a few fantastic ebooks and guides which were manufactured by sexologists and sex pros with huge knowledge in these things, you'll find a person. The real key to optimizing and learning the way to talk dirty is based on understanding what it's and receiving the ideal measures or guide to follow along.

Since men are very different, you've got to get out what your individual enjoys and that which he doesn't like. If you're a timid woman, then you should start simple using sweet words and messages that are flirty. If your man is off, you're able to cause the mood by sending him sexy flirting and messages on the device. This, in case it moves well, if you put the mood for suitable gender, start the lines of communication and assist you in building confidence. If it has to do with the true sexual activity, that is the point where you need to call the inner slut inside you.

There are various sorts of phrases you may utilize. The ideal start is to share with your man the best way to are feeling and dig the feelings and feelings flowing through the human entire body. The other sort of filthy conversation is to tell him exactly what you would like him to accomplish - it may be the way to motivate you personally, the way you can squeeze your brow, or exactly what to whisper to your ear. The 3rd type of filthy conversation is reassuring your man farther and also to inform him exactly what he can right.

One of things which may intensify gender - or sometimes completely murder that the mood is filthy discussing. There are various degrees of naughtiness - a few types of filthy speaking are fantastic for a few while other hardcore types of filthy speaking can well not move so well with everybody else. You have to admit, in the event that you watched the scandalous sexts and raunchy images that olivia munn provided for her former boyfriend chris pine, then you had been kind of astonished on merely hoe gloomy and dirty individuals are able to get. The language she had was so hardcore I can't share it.

The significant question would be, where's the line which divides dirty talking - the one that's so competitive that it transforms him into a tiger - and the only plain dirt which would possibly be turn away? I did a little research and came back up with a couple dirty conversation guidelines about which guys thing concerning various dirty-talk phrases. These traces have been independently billed and certainly will steer you to comprehend exactly what exactly lines have been erotically charged and those that are a nono in any way times.

Girl says, "I would like one to continue moving your tongue just like this."

Boy believes: "if a girl gives me guidelines, this means she's receptive and wants me to learn what amuses her and that I may well soon be glad to oblige. I've already been having enough girls to learn each has her tender stains, of course, when she disturbs me in an ideal way, it conserves time and a great deal of disappointments."

Girl says, "any word which has the word 'daddy'."

Boy thinks: "this really is an enormous turn away. If she says that the word 'daddy,' my mind instantly flashbacks in dad, also at this type of circumstance, probably something that I may possibly have seen him perform with mom, also now there goes my own erection. In any case, any word using"daddy" may possibly turn out as absurd."

Girl claims: "share with me quicker and more difficult infant."

Lady thinks: "that really is sexy, particularly during the heat of this moment if heads are lost from each other's' universe; however, it comes off because of porn-star-ish. In case she wants faster and harder, she should perhaps not be let down in case it finishes up a tad too."

Girl claims: "any filthy phrases using a solid f and words."

Boy thinks: "this is a twist on when I had been on the job, and you're waiting in your home. But if we're only starting, it better be sexy and wet - do not state it is. Guys can say so when he is expecting finds and slippery out its dry, it might be such a turn away."

Getting hardcore

Up to now, we've mentioned nearly exactly what you will need to get going down the filthy talk street. If you aren't there yet, you are well on the path from today, and you also could be getting curious by what's next. What happens once you might be much more familiar with filthy conversation, and you are in the mood to maneuver out of one's safe place? You obtain a hardcore, baby. Becoming into hardcore dreams frequently means language that is hardcore. It may be really hard to locate the correct words to spell out what's on the mind; however, it may be accomplished. It simply requires some imagination and plenty of minds. Being fully truthful along with your partner will soon start wide horizons of this hardcore character! Bear in mind those internet hunts you did when you're thinking about talking dirty for your partner? Now's a fantastic time to return back into people. You are becoming better about talking dirty, and it's really getting increasingly more spontaneous; however, your language can expand to include items that surprise him make his libido increase. Return straight back again to all those porn videos, those which you watched when you're getting thoughts for filthy conversation. See them, however, bring your seasoned ear. Words that did not direct you before may well light your flames today. As you see, consider what your partner says for you personally, and also how he responds to a voice. Those that could visit his cause? Return straight back and pick those up sensual books, too. Bear in mind the short stories which were so sexy they have the party started until you struck page 5? Return straight back again to people and examine the stories you simply deemed "a lot of" during that time you purchased the publication. How can you experience these today that you have had an opportunity to learn more about the kingdom of filthy conversation a little more? Bring your partner in on your own mind. Games for couples are almost always good, why don't you start there? Sitting completely straightened on your bedroom, then start with throwing words out. Challenge him to think of something sexier. As an example, you may say "thrusting," and he would cancel with "stroking." insert a growing number of words, and soon you're showering one another with naughtiness. Does this allow you to glow? Does this make you laugh? Good! If you are laughing and breathing harder and handing each other, which coy look, which means that which you understand this indicates, which usually means you are becoming familiar with the notion of this hard-core dirty conversation phrases. This may possibly be a very good time to inquire that words turn on. Asking when you are at a relaxed, serene feeling, still fully dressed, will be taking off the sensual pressure. It provides you with an opportunity to actually think of the language you've already been using and also how you are feeling about these. By way of instance, he may have called you a "bitch" during sex yesterday, and you also were astonished that it turned out you. However, you'd never wish to get called such a name out the sack because it'd have a completely different connotation. Now's the opportunity to create those up gaps and chat about them with your partner; thus, there isn't any question about that which is fine and what's not. Below are a number of phrases to think about. How can you experience these? I really like your big, sexy dick. Your penis is ideal for my own pussy. This pussy is yours to fuck, isn't it? Would you like to buy it, not? Take which encounter my hot, wet cunt. Give it to me personally, you sexy bastard. Fuck me harder. Faster. You prefer it if I am giving you my encounter, not? Suck it out of me. You would like to fuck my tits along with your pole? Make me gag on your penis. You prefer it if your bitch rides on your dick, not? All that discuss filthy conversation only can lead to still another heated encounter. As it will, employ the newest factors, you've heard, and also, you shouldn't be reluctant to branch out to matters which may turn you into just a little uneasy. Assessing your bounds is a fantastic thing, and may result in the type of gloomy conversation that could cause some of the porn celebrities to blush! Bear in mind those dreams we spoke about earlier in this publication? The hardcore dreams, which may force you to say, "whoaback up a little there!" You might realize that you simply like some of the dreams, along with your dirty-talk, may possibly begin to signify that. Should it, think that you may possibly like to go further into a hardcore talk, and start throwing out words and phrases which may shock you. In reality, try out some of them on for size. Are you prepared to proceed this way? Take the jism around my fucking pussy. I am gont consume buckets from one's spooge, and after that, you're planning to lick at it out of my tongue. You would like to suck on my dick after I have fucked your bum, you dirty whore? I will ride you want a motherfucking jack-hammer. Lick your encounter out of the pussy. Can it, pussy boy. I will blow it up to your bum. Suck my balls once I encounter in your own clit. Can it. Get there. Think I will simply take your entire hand up my slutty cunt? Let us discover. Spank who pussy, you bad boy. That is only the tip of this iceberg with the dirty, dirty conversation you may wind coming from your own mouth. Whenever you are too hot to watch directly, there isn't any telling exactly what you could state. Some of your deepest, wildest dreams are certain to turn out. And that's an excellent thing! Let us go back once more for all those hardcore dreams. Sometimes, dirty-talk is not enough...sometimes, you want a little additional pep to discover where you will need to be using a severe role-playing game. And how can you do so, you ask? Simple. Sextoys! It's possible to meet a few of the fantasies with the assistance of interesting and dependable sex toys. As an example, if your enthusiast said just how far he'd like to see that you fuck another man while he sees, create it happen -- even figuratively. Opt for a dildo which resembles a person's manhood, and next time he cites that specific dream, introduce him into a fresh toy. With a couple well-placed words, then you may place the hard-core point for a dream which may blow him off! An alternative will function as"a lot more than one woman" dream. You may get this happen to have a pocket pussya tiny masturbator that's intended to feel and look much like a lady's anus. Blind fold him or her scale together with him settling your pussy on his face, so when he is into what you are doing to each other, then introduce the sex-toy by him/her how far you'd really like to satisfy this dream and also watch him along with other females. Twist the pocket pussy down his dick...and you're able to simply take all of it out there! These would be the simplest types of what you could do in order to add your dirty-talk and gender toys right into hardcore drama with. The chances are endless! Just continue to keep the communication going and also the closeness living, and also, your cluttered chat encounter will be described as a magnificent, yelling success!

CPSIA information can be obtained
at www.ICGtesting.com
Printed in the USA
BVHW041722060621
609091BV00016B/2581